Orthodoxy for Children

Fr. Anthony Borisov

Prayer

**Illustrations by
Anastasia Novik**

Grand Rapids · Exaltation Press · 2019

Copyright © 2019 Exaltation Press

Author: Fr. Anthony Borisov
Illustrator: Anastasia Novik
Translator: Fr. John Hogg

"Prayer"

     Prayer is at the heart of our Christian life. As parents, one of our main tasks is to teach our children how to pray, to bring them to our Lord, and to teach them to turn to Him in all of life's joys and sorrows. This book is designed as a support for parents who are trying to be faithful in this great task.

All rights reserved. This book or any portion thereof may not be reproduced or used in any manner whatsoever without the express written permission of the publisher except for the use of brief quotations in a book review.

Translated from the original "О Молитве" by Nikea Press, Copyright © Trading house «NIKEA», www.Nikeabooks.ru

ISBN: 978-1-950067-91-6 (Paperback)

Edited by Cynthia Hogg

First printing edition 2019

Exaltation Press
Grand Rapids, MI

www.ExaltationPress.com

For bulk orders, please contact editor@exaltationpress.com.

Table of Contents

CONVERSATION 4

GOD IS NEAR 6

HOW TO TALK WITH GOD 8

PRAYER OF THE HEART 10

WHY SHOULD WE PRAY? 12

MY FIRST PRAYER 14

WHICH PRAYER IS THE MOST IMPORTANT? 16

WHEN DOES GOD NOT HEAR OUR PRAYERS? 18

WHAT IF THE PRAYERS HAVE UNFAMILIAR WORDS? 20

PRAYER WITHOUT WORDS 22

IS IT BETTER TO PRAY AT HOME OR AT CHURCH? 24

PRAYING IN FRONT OF AN ICON 26

PRAYER TO THE SAINTS 28

LITURGY: OUR COMMON PRAYER 30

PRAYING FOR OTHER PEOPLE 32

CONVERSATION

Isn't it wonderful that we have phones? Whenever you want, you can call or write your mom or dad, or a friend. You can share with them what's going on in your life, both the good and the not-so-good. It's amazing to get to talk to someone you're close to, who listens to you, supports you, and participates in your life. Can you imagine how hard it is for people who don't have that ability? It's not that they don't have a phone but rather that they have no one to call. Sometimes there are people who have no close friends and no relatives. Their lives are filled with loneliness. That loneliness fills everything with emptiness and silence. It seems there's no way out. Believe me, though, there is!

> An old man stood motionless in a corner of a church for hours on end. He wasn't just standing. You could see that he was praying.
> Once, the priest asked the old man what God was saying.
> "God isn't saying anything. He's just listening," the old man answered.
> "Well, then what are you saying to Him?"
> "I'm not saying anything either. I'm listening to Him."

> "Happy are those who are in touch with Heaven!"
>
> *St. Paisius of Mt. Athos*

5 Prayer

GOD IS NEAR

Sometimes, we get disappointed with people, even those closest to us. A friend unexpectedly refuses to help you. Your parents promise to take you to go see a movie but then aren't able to, even though you were really looking forward to it. After disappointment, loneliness comes knocking at our heart. But there is Someone that will never leave you, who will not let sadness seize your heart. That someone is God. The Lord loves us all very much. His love is very tender and devoted. His love never ends. Unlike people, God always keeps His promises. He will never leave you alone. Even if there's no one near you, even if the phone doesn't ring, God is always near you.

Once, a man dreamed that he was walking along a sandy beach and the Lord was near him. Before him, he saw scenes from his life and he noticed that there were two sets of footprints in the sand, one from his feet and the other from the Lord's feet. In some places, though, there was only one set of footprints. The man remembered that those were the most difficult and unhappy times in his life. He was very sad and asked the Lord, "Why did you leave me when I needed you the most?" The Lord answered "My child, I love you and I will never leave you. During the times of grief and sadness, there is only one set of footprints in the sand because that was when I carried you in My arms."

7 Prayer

HOW TO TALK WITH GOD

> Once, a priest was visiting a family. Before lunch, he said, "The father of the family should say grace because he is the chief intercessor for his own family." There was an uncomfortable silence because usually no one in the family prayed. The father said, "We don't say grace because the prayer is so repetitive. It's always the same thing. Repetitive prayer is just empty words." The priest looked at them all with surprise but then their seven-year-old daughter said, "Dad, does that mean that I shouldn't come and say good morning to you anymore?"

Many adults believe in science, or rather, what they call science but which is really just their own conviction: if you can't see or feel something, that means it doesn't exist. Some people even say the same thing about God. "I don't see or hear Him. That means He doesn't exist!" It's easy to see that isn't true. All we need to do is to turn to God in prayer. If we sincerely ask God for help, ask Him for guidance, or give Him thanks for something, He always answers us. When talking to God, there's a little secret. The Lord talks to us only in the ways we're ready to hear Him. The saints talk to him face-to-face. Many of us, however, aren't ready for that and so God interacts with us through the circumstances of our lives, through other people, and sometimes by sending good thoughts and desires into our hearts.

9 Prayer

PRAYER OF THE HEART

When we pray, we often use words. We either ask God for something or else thank Him for answering our prayers. But prayer is more than just words. If our prayers were just words, they would lose their meaning. Imagine calling your mom on the phone. You're telling her something but you're distracted and not really paying attention. Your conversation would become empty, mere words. There would be no warmth. Your heart wouldn't really be in the conversation. Do you know how offensive that is to someone? If we pray with words only, without putting our minds and hearts into the prayer, God does not receive that kind of prayer, since it is only words that don't really mean anything special to us.

> This story happened in a small village. It was the middle of summer and there was a drought. The priest called all the people to church to pray for rain. The whole village came and they all laughed at a little boy who had come with an umbrella. "What a foolish child! Why did you come with an umbrella? There's no rain!" "Well," the boy said, "I thought that if we pray, the rain will come."

11 Prayer

WHY SHOULD WE PRAY?

When I was studying in seminary (a school for future priests), I had to pray with the other students every morning and evening. I remember that some of us complained, saying that prayer shouldn't just be done on a fixed schedule. I also wondered about that. I asked an old priest what he thought about praying on a schedule. His answer surprised me. He told me that prayer isn't meant to be a burden. It should be like a conversation with your parents who you've been missing. When he said that, I remembered that while in seminary, I did call home every day at the same time, as it happened. But even though it was on a fixed schedule, those calls brought joy both to my mother and me. From then on, prayer for me was like calling home, to my Heavenly Father, and no longer felt like a burden.

"Only one who does not really want to pray is unable to find time to pray."

St. Innocent of Alaska, Metropolitan of Moscow

Prayer

MY FIRST PRAYER

I remember very well when prayer first entered my life. My grandmother taught me to pray. She was born and grew up in a little village so the words of her prayers were simple but sincere. She taught me a prayer about the Cross of Christ. When I repeat the words of the prayer, I remember what I thought back then. I thought how difficult it must have been for Jesus Christ to live in our world, to carry the heavy cross of the sins of others. I remember wanting to help Him a little, to help Him carry that heavy burden. When I said the words of that simple village prayer, I felt that I was close to Him. My soul became light and easy.

O Father of Mankind! Heavenly Father! May Your eternal Name shine through our hearts! May Your Kingdom come! May Your will be done with us on earth like it is in Heaven! Send down our daily bread with Your generous hand. Just like we forgive others, so forgive us, Your worthless children, O Father. Do not plunge us into temptation but deliver us from the evil deceiver and have mercy on us!

Alexander Pushkin

Our Father who art in heaven, Hallowed be thy name. Thy kingdom come. Thy will be done on earth as it is in heaven. Give us this day our daily bread, and forgive us our trespasses, as we forgive those who trespass against us, and lead us not into temptation, but deliver us from the evil one.

15 Prayer

WHICH PRAYER IS THE MOST IMPORTANT?

> Once, a young man was asked, "What do you think? Is there some prayer that is more important and necessary than the others?" "Of course there is!" he replied immediately. "It is the prayer that the Lord Himself taught us, the 'Our Father.'" Which words of the prayer are the most important?" "Thy will be done." "Why those words?" they asked him. "Because we never know what is really best for us, what is most beneficial. That is why we ask that the Lord's will be done with us, just like it is in Heaven."

This question probably seems strange to you. Did you know, however, that this is a prayer that wasn't just written by a human being, but by God Himself? The name of the prayer comes from its first two words, "Our Father." Jesus Christ, our Savior, was the first to pray this prayer, when His Apostles asked Him to teach them. The Apostles were simple fishermen, without much education. They wanted to know the right way to talk to God. Christ gave them this prayer. It begins with an amazing expression – "Our Father." Before Christ, we wouldn't have dared to call God our Father. The Savior showed us that God loves us just like a father. That is why we can now call Him "our Father."

17 Prayer

WHEN DOES GOD NOT HEAR OUR PRAYERS?

There are times when God doesn't hear our prayers. When this happens, it isn't because God is stubborn or doesn't have enough time for us. Not at all. God doesn't answer our prayers if we are angry at someone and refuse to forgive them. Do you remember how we explained that prayer isn't just what we say with our lips? True prayer comes first and foremost from our heart. What do you think? Can a heart that is overcome with resentment really pray well? Does the Lord enjoy talking to a heart like that? If we want God to hear our prayers, we need to live in peace within ourselves and with the people around us. We need to learn to forgive and not hold onto grudges. If we do, our communion with God will never be broken.

Once there was a monk who had been greatly wronged by someone. He went to the monastery's elder and said, "Someone wronged me and I want to get revenge." The elder answered him, "No, my son, let God Himself be the judge of everything. You must forgive the person who wronged you." But the monk couldn't find any peace. Then, the elder said, "Let's pray to God together." While they were praying, the elder begin to say out loud, "O God! We no longer need You. From now on, we ourselves will judge other people and get vengance for our wrongs!" When he heard this, the monk was frightened. He understood his mistake and said, "Forgive me! God is dearer to me than anything else. If I must choose between the Lord and getting revenge, I will forgive the one who wronged me. I will not get revenge."

Prayer

> "If you do not even hear your own prayers (because you are distracted), how do you expect God to hear them?"
>
> *St. John Chrysostom*

WHAT IF THE PRAYERS HAVE UNFAMILIAR WORDS?

Sometimes in Church, the words that are used can sound old and hard to understand. Don't give up, though! The words that you see in prayers are not so very different from the words that you use. It will only be at the beginning that the words seem hard to understand. If you come to Church regularly and sing and pray along and if you say your prayers at home, you will soon get used to them and begin to understand them and see the beauty in them. That doesn't mean, however, that you can't pray to God in your own words. God knows and understands all languages. So when you say your personal prayers, you can use the words that are closest to your heart.

"We can talk to God just like we would talk to another person. He understands every language. He understands the movements of our souls. He knows everything."

Patriarch Kyrill of Moscow

"O God! Make the bad people good and make the good people kind!"

A little girl's prayer

21 Prayer

PRAYER WITHOUT WORDS

Did you know that prayer doesn't always need words? There are situations when words aren't needed. There are movements that can be prayers. The most well-known is the Sign of the Cross. From the earliest days of the Church, Christians marked themselves with the Cross. That was a way for them to pray to God without words. Over time, the exact way we cross ourselves has changed. Now, the way we make the Sign of the Cross is by folding the fingers of our right hand like this: we put our pinky finger and ring finger on our palm and then join our thumb, index finger, and middle finger together. By folding our fingers like that, we express our faith that God is the Trinity and that Christ has two natures -- He is both God and Man. Once we have folded our fingers, we cross ourselves by touching our forehead, stomach, and shoulders. When we cross ourselves, we ask God to sanctify us and to give us pure thoughts and bodily strength.

> Once there lived a monk in Russia who was all by himself in a small hut. One day, some people stumbled upon his little house and asked the monk, "How do you have the patience to live by yourself deep in the forest?" The monk answered with a smile, "I'm not alone! I have someone to talk to - the Lord. When I want Him to talk to me, I read the Bible, the Holy Scriptures that God gave to mankind. When I want to talk to Him, I pray. He always hears me."

23 Prayer

IS IT BETTER TO PRAY AT HOME OR AT CHURCH?

Do you remember that we said that prayer is a conversation, a conversation between us and God? I'm sure you understand that there are different ways of talking to someone. For example, if you want to talk to someone, you can call them on the phone or you can go visit them. If you talk to them on the phone, you will only hear their voice but if you go to see them, it will be different. The conversation will be fuller and more complete. Prayer is like that. Of course, the Lord is overjoyed to hear the prayers we say at home. He's even more happy, though, when we come to visit Him, when we go to Church. The Church is, after all, the house of God. The Church is where we can feel His presence most clearly. We should definitely pray at home (every morning and evening) but we should never forget to go to Church. The Lord is inviting you to be His guest. Someone with good manners would never turn down an invitation like that!

> A fisherman was giving someone a ride in his boat. The passenger saw that on one paddle was written "Pray!" and on the other "Work!" He asked the fisherman why. "To help me remember," the fisherman answered. "So that I don't forget that I should always work and pray." "Well, I understand why you need to work. But prayer... that isn't really necessary. Nobody needs your prayers. Why waste time on prayer?" "It's not necessary?" the fisherman asked and then pulled the paddle that said "Pray!" out of the water and started to row with just one paddle. The boat went in circles. "You see? That is what work is like without prayer. We spin around in place and cannot move forward."

25 Prayer

PRAYING IN FRONT OF AN ICON

As you have already realized, the Church isn't just a building, but the house of God. When you go in, you will understand that the Lord really lives there. It isn't just a matter of our inward feelings. In the Church, you will see icons, images of God and the saints. An icon isn't just a picture. It is a "window" into the spiritual world – the world where the angels and saints reside. There are icons in Church for a reason. The first icon was made by the Apostle Luke. It was an icon of the Mother of Jesus Christ, the Virgin Mary. Later, other icons appeared with images of other saints. Christians believe that icons do not just show us the outside, but the person of a saint in its fullness. When we pray in front of an icon, we come into contact with the spiritual world. We enter into communion with God and His saints.

> Everything can change in such a miraculous way when we ask for God's help. Pray to God to help you with your homework, to be with you at school, to help you get along with your teachers and the other students. Believe me, He will answer your prayer. Maybe not right away. But what do we value more? Things that happen right away or things that we get slowly? The second, of course! Pray to God and He will take care of everything. But don't be lazy yourself!

> "Rublev's icon of the Trinity exists and therefore, so does God."
>
> *Fr. Pavel Florensky*

PRAYER TO THE SAINTS

We not only pray to God but also to holy people, the saints. Saints are people whose lives were an example of love for God and others, who lived their lives in mercy and care for their neighbors. Orthodox Christians especially love to pray to the Most-holy Theotokos, the mother of the Savior of the world, Jesus Christ. A long time ago, there were some people who didn't understand prayer to the saints. They began to doubt that it was okay to pray to the saints. They thought that it made God seem not as important. However, there isn't really anything wrong with prayer to the saints. The saints don't take the place of God for us but only add their prayers to ours and make them stronger. When we talk to the saints, we aren't really praying to them but praying with them to the Lord. We pray to God here on Earth and they supplement our prayers with their own prayers in Heaven.

> All of us, each and everyone one, have our own talents and vocation! The saints understand that very well. They also understand, though, that without God, it is hard to achieve anything good. When the saints didn't have strength of their own, they asked for God's strength. They asked for wisdom and inspiration, and then kept working diligently. And everything worked out in the end. They became spiritual teachers for many people and warmed them with their love, saved them from perishing, and led them to faith. They are still doing that even now.

Prayer

LITURGY: OUR COMMON PRAYER

There is one kind of prayer that can't be said alone. When Christ lived in our world, He gave His disciples and apostles a command. The Savior asked them to come together to pray and remember His life and death. That common prayer developed into a whole service, called Liturgy, which is a Greek word that means "a common work." At Liturgy, the priest prays together with all of the parishioners. Together, they remember Christ's great and saving work. It is during Liturgy that the greatest Mystery of the Church takes place - Holy Communion, when the bread and wine mystically become the Body and Blood of Christ. This miracle only takes place when we are assembled together for prayer. You can take part in this miracle whenever you come to Liturgy.

A Prayer of Thanksgiving After Communion

"May Thy holy Body, O Lord Jesus Christ our God, be to me for eternal life and Thy precious Blood for the forgiveness of my sins. May this Eucharist be to me for joy, health, and gladness."

31 Prayer

PRAYING FOR OTHER PEOPLE

When we pray, we don't only ask God for our own needs. We believe that a true Christian cannot live just for himself or herself. Christ calls us to show mercy and love to other people. Of course, we have to express that love and mercy in our actions. We need to wash the dishes, tidy up the house, help others carry their bags. These little, simple actions are actually very important. They show our true feelings to those around us. Praying for others is also an expression of love for them. When you turn to God in prayer with your requests, please don't forget about others who also need God's help. Pray to God for your parents, your grandparents, and your friends. Pray also for those who you might not like very much. I understand that it can be difficult. But if you do it, if you pray for them, then the Lord will never forget your prayers, but will receive them with joy.

www.ingramcontent.com/pod-product-compliance
Lightning Source LLC
Chambersburg PA
CBHW051351110526
44591CB00025B/2964